Tim

Written by John Lockyer
Illustrated by Raymond McGrath

PEARSON

"Don't struggle!" shouted a rough voice.

But Tonk did struggle. Dropping his satchel, he kicked and jerked. It was no use. Thick arms were squeezing the breath from him. He dropped to the ground under a heavy heap of sour-smelling sacking.

What was happening? He'd crossed the park hundreds of times before. It was the way home from the Learning Centre. The park was safe. Everywhere on Chulo was safe.

Tonk felt dizzy. Suddenly, the weight shifted and the foul sacking was scratched off his face. Gasping, he saw a head with wild red eyes, scraggly hair, chipped teeth and scaly skin. He wanted to shout for help but could only gag.

The strange being grabbed Tonk's tunic. "Get up. Don't run," it said, crossing its glowing metal hands.

The voice sounded old and far away. And the hand crossing... It's some sort of language decoding system, Tonk thought.

He stood shakily beside the pathway, trapped between a pile of stones and thick trees. The strange being shuffled closer.

Tonk caught a whiff of the stench again. Its clothes were matted with grime. Glowing, metal, toeless feet protruded from open boots. Its hairless arms were scaled. Its ears, eyes, nose and hair were skewed, as if each feature had been plonked hurriedly in its place.

Tonk knew the being didn't come from Earth and it didn't belong on Chulo. He watched its eyes shift down to the dial on his wrist.

"Give it to me!" it said, crossing its hands again.

Tonk shook his head.

"Give it or I'll take it."

Tonk shook his head again and stepped back. He felt branches jab into him. He had to explain. He held up his arm, flashing the dial, showing his holographic image floating beneath the transparent cover.

"This is my life preserver. All Chulo inhabitants wear one. Chulo is an Earth satellite but has greater air pressure. The preserver creates an Earth-like pressure membrane around me. Without the preserver, I'll implode and die."

Tonk looked for a similar life-preserving device on the being, but there wasn't one. It had to be protected in another way. "You don't need one to exist here?"

The being pointed both hands at the dial. "With the preserver, I can complete the quest."

Tonk frowned. "Quest?"

"I'm a tunnel dweller from another world. I live and work underground, building and cleaning city waste tunnels. Sometimes scientists visit the tunnels to get volunteer time travellers. I am a volunteer."

Keep it talking, Tonk thought. "But a preserver might be useless in your world."

The traveller gave a smile, or perhaps it was a grimace. "We have no true inventors. Our scientists are imitators. If a traveller returns with something useful, they copy it, or parts of it. Unfortunately, the copies are never as good as the originals. I am an example... But it is how our world progresses."

The traveller closed its eyes. "The reward for finding something like the preserver is freedom. When I return, I will leave the tunnels to live above ground in wonderful fresh air and light."

Tonk heard three faint beeps… The traveller's eyes snapped open. **"Time is up."**

Tonk suddenly felt cold. "Delay your return," he said desperately.

"Impossible. It is pre-programmed."

"Then choose something else." Tonk emptied his pockets. "My piezo multi-tool... my personal data card. It will give you entry to Earth. Earth has thousands… no, millions of useful things."

The traveller shook its head.

Tonk stared into the park, searching for help, but there was none. The traveller grabbed his wrist and wrenched it upwards. Tonk wriggled free. He wouldn't give in. Twisting around to shield his arm with his body, he had a glimmer of an idea. It flitted around the edge of his mind… something about time… something he had learned at the centre?

Finally the idea took shape. Tonk straightened up, raised his hands above his head and shouted, "Wait! The objects that volunteers bring to your world — are they from the past or the future?"

The traveller didn't answer. It reached for the preserver again and Tonk twisted away again.

"Without the preserver, I'm dead! Tell me, please.
Do volunteers collect things from the past or the future?"

The traveller seemed to frown. "Always from the past. I am the first future time traveller."

Tonk relaxed. "I must warn you. The workings of time travel won't let you take back any information that might change future happenings. Your memory of this visit will be blank."

The traveller grabbed Tonk's arm. "I don't want information. I **want** the preserver."

He ripped it free and Tonk immediately collapsed under an immense, invisible force. The skin on his face sucked inwards. His heart slowed. His breath wheezed. He was dying, but he wasn't afraid.

Above him, the traveller held the preserver in its metal hands. Its red eyes sparked. It gave a shudder, a croaky snort and began to fade.

Tonk kept his eyes fixed on the preserver. While the traveller slowly vanished, it stayed complete. Tonk heard a sharp crack. The traveller was gone, but the preserver hung in the air for a moment, then fell to the ground.

Tonk reached for it. The small movement took enormous effort. His mouth opened, but he couldn't breathe. His heart fluttered as he clasped the preserver to his wrist. He closed his eyes and lay still.

A noise awakened him. It was a low sound of people talking and walking along the path. Tonk didn't call out. Unharmed, he got quietly to his feet and brushed himself down.

He stared up at the sky. "Your world has a lot to learn. All time... past and future... is moving forward. As you know, travellers into the past can return to their world with anything, including memories, because the past is part of present time. But you didn't know that travellers into the future can only return to their world exactly as they left it. The future is not part of present time. Everything is stripped from future travellers as they move back against the flow of time."

Tonk picked up his satchel and glanced at the sky again. "I'm sorry you have to stay in the tunnels but, if I had told you it was impossible to take the preserver, you might have thrown it away or destroyed it. To stay safe, I had to make sure it was always in my reach."

What is Science Fiction?

Time Quest is **Science Fiction**.

Science fiction is a narrative in which the author uses scientific language and ideas to write about an imaginary, futuristic world.

A science-fiction story has a **plot** with:

- **an introduction**
- **a problem**
- **a resolution.**

How to Write a Science Fiction Story

Step 1

Make a *story plan* to help you organise your story.

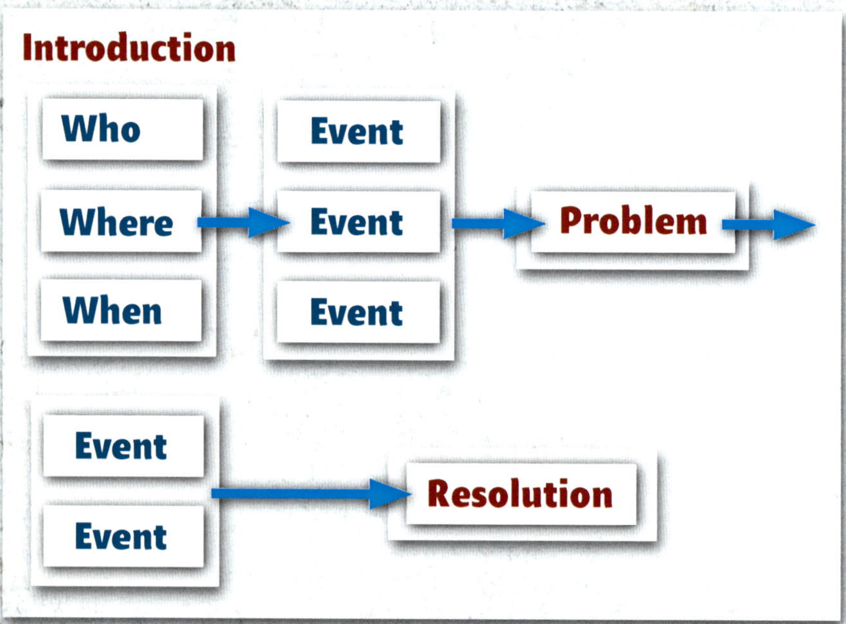

Step 2

Look back at your plan and write an *introduction*, using:

- *characters* from the future
- a *setting* in a futuristic, imaginary world
- *scientific words*: time traveller, Chulo, decoding system, holographic image, preserver, pressure membrane

Step 3

Write about the *events* of the story that *led up* to the *problem*.

Step 4

Write about *what happens* as a *result* of the events, i.e. the *problem*.

Step 5

Write about the *sequence of events* that lead to the *resolution*.

Step 6

Write about the *resolution*. Tell the reader *how* the problem was resolved.

Guide Notes

Title: Time Quest
Stage: Advanced Fluency
Text Form: Science Fiction
Approach: Guided Reading
Processes: Thinking Critically, Exploring Language, Processing Information
Written and Visual Focus: Illustrative Text

Thinking Critically

(sample questions)

- Look at the cover and title page. What text form do you think this book will be?
- Look at pages 2-3. What is your opinion about the introduction to this story? Do you think readers will want to read on? Why or why not?
- Look at pages 4-5. How effectively has the author described the strange being that has captured Tonk? What helped your visualisation of this character?
- Look at pages 6-7. How has the author used scientific language and ideas to create the imaginary, futuristic world so far?
- Look at pages 8-9. What feelings do you think the author wants to evoke when he writes about the traveller's life underground and his desire for freedom to "live above ground in wonderful fresh air and light"?
- Look at pages 10-11. What inferences can you make about Tonk from the way he is dealing with the traveller?
- Look at pages 12-13. From what you know about the traveller, how do you think it will respond to Tonk's information about time travel and the way it works?
- Look at pages 14-15. What inferences can you make about what will happen to the traveller now?
- Do you think the resolution to this story is credible? Why or why not?
- What questions do you have about this text?
- Who would you recommend this story to and why?

Exploring Language

Vocabulary

Clarify: satchel, sour-smelling, gag, language decoding system, protruded, matted with grime, skewed, feature, holographic image, membrane, implode, grimace, wrenched, immense
Synonyms: Discuss synonyms for *sour, stench, protruded, implode*
Antonyms: Discuss antonyms for *sour, safe, imitators*
Simile: *as if each feature had been plonked hurriedly in its place*